Ban The Bark

How to resolve excessive barking issues at home

Jo Loft IMDT

Peer Reviews

I have known Jo for many years and followed her dog training journey with many dogs as she worked hard to set up her successful canine business, Paws-itivity. Ban the Bark is the perfect book for anyone wanting to stop their dog from barking excessively and who wants to learn how to do this using a clear, simple and proven method, based always on positive reward. The book is written in easy to understand style with added humour making it a fun read as well as an informative one. The exercises to teach your dogs outlined in this book, cover some essential basic behaviours that all dogs need be taught; it addresses far more that stopping your dog from barking. Excellent value for money.

Sue Dennison -FdSc Animal Behaviour & Welfare. Behavioural consultant and dog trainer

Testimonials for Ban the Bark

Jo has a wealth of experience and knowledge of dogs- training, behaviour, well-being, bonding, mental stimulation, and ways to just have fun together. I signed up for the 'Ban the Bark' course for my older Sprocker who always wants to voice her opinion. The course was excellent with videos, print outs, and live tutorials. Jo had the time to tailor training to each dog and their own bark triggers. Our house is quieter and I have the confidence that you CAN teach an old dog new tricks. Whatever your problem, Jo will try to find a way to help and support you- and she loves celebrating your successes.
M Ridout

Ban the bark was easy to follow due to the way Jo structured the course. She explains everything so clearly and always answered any questions we had. Our little dog, Dylan, thrives on her positive reinforcement training methods and the improvement in him is amazing!
T Stayton

Not only do you understand dogs, you are equally good at understanding their owners. You put so much into every one of us it is not surprising how much dogs and people like you. Your approach is like a breath of fresh air; every session is like a one-to-one session. The extras you do are great fun and your training videos are a must watch: light, fun, entertaining so motivating that we can't wait to have a go. Thank you!
P Wells

The testimonials and examples within this book are from students that have attended my Ban the Bark online course April 2020 and are not a guarantee of your success as this will vary for each individual's circumstances.

For all my dog's past, present and future. You continue to teach me so much; you ask for nothing but give me everything.

Strive for progress, not perfection

Contents

Foreword then forwards

If you have purchased this book, then you are one of many dog owners that experience the frustrating and noisy habit of excessive barking at home.

We love our dogs greatly, but there is nothing worse than relaxing or working at home to then be bombarded with a sudden explosion of expletives from our dogs. Then it seems that once they have found their barking mojo, they are more attuned to really letting the world know their opinion about a situation.

There are a variety of reasons your dog may be barking excessively and this book will help you to get to the root of the problem and will help you work towards a resolution - resulting in a much quieter and more relaxed dog at home, no matter what causes your dog to bark.

All the information in this book can easily be adapted to suit your situation and your dog. There are lots of things to consider before working on a behaviour adjustment program, and before doing so you should ensure that there is no medical reason that will hinder your results or affect your dog further.

The methods and training tools in this book are not intended for use with dogs barking due to separation anxiety: this is an entirely different issue and help and advice should be sought through your local qualified behaviourist.

This book will teach you how to use positive reinforcement to train your dog with no aversive exercises or aids. This program was originally provided online, but due to its success it has been made more widely available. While the exercises within this book have been described to help you resolve problem and excessive barking, success cannot be guaranteed.

Resolving a training problem is dependent on many factors including the person doing the training and the individual dog.

Information provided in this book is in no way to be used to diagnose a behavioural or medical problem. You should seek advice from professionals who are licenced and certified, do not disregard their advice because of my opinions in this book.

Throughout this book I have written referring to dogs as him, he or his to represent both sexes. It is not reflecting a gender bias but used for convenience when writing.

Acknowledgements

As always, there are many dogs and people to thank for the creation of this program. Firstly, to all the dogs I have owned and worked with, that constantly teach me how to be better.

To all my Ban the Bark students past and present that have helped to bring this book to fruition with all your positivity, enjoyment and successes.

To my mother for supporting me throughout the whole transition from rat race to dog's pace, without her I would not be where I am today.

To Helen for mentoring me every week with help, advice, and a positive approach to all things dog.

To Mick who pushed me to take the leap, I knew I should have done it years sooner, but I would never have done it at all if it were not for you.

To Sue for your sage advice and support throughout our canine careers has been invaluable, whether puppy or problematic pooch, you have been there to lend a helping hand.

To Dom (The Pet Biz Wiz) for encouraging the transition from online course to published book.

Finally, to you, for purchasing this book. This is the first step to working on the issue of excessive barking. When you finally realise that something needs to change, you can commit to make changes.

My inspiration for this book

I currently have four dogs, all terrier mixes. Those of you with terrier mixes will understand that I need to be alerted to passers-by, knocks at doors, loud vehicles passing as well as birds and butterflies in the garden.

The more I worked from home typing reports, designing courses and lesson plans, the more I realised how much my fluffers were barking. If one started, the others would join in and this canine chorus would rise to a long lasting crescendo.

Therefore, finally taking the time to resolve the matter of my own fluffers excessive barking turned out to be one of the best things I've ever done; which is why I have had to share it with you.

Throughout this book there are lots of areas to work on, but please remember to look at your training journey as a marathon and not a sprint.

Do not aim straight for the end goal, that will come in time, instead work on small manageable chunks that are easily achievable and ensure you are always setting your dog up for success.

"Strive for progress not perfection"
David Perlmutter

The main thing I want you to take on board is setting your dog up for success, do not shoot straight for the stars, that is unachievable and you will only be setting you and your dog up for failure, which is not fair on either of you.

This book will help you to look at your situation in carefully structured units that you can work through in your own time and move to the next unit when you are happy and ready to do so.

Remember that training should be fun for you and your dog: you are a team. If you find yourself overwhelmed, then take a step back and revisit areas you are comfortable with. I know from my own experience that this is a tough journey, but you've got this.

IMPORTANT

No matter how much training you have done with your dog, no matter how good a dog owner/trainer you believe you are, the behaviours you have CAN always be better. Which is why as you progress through this book the one thing you should keep at the forefront of your mind is – The 3Ds.

When you start teaching a behaviour (any behaviour) it should be done in a controlled environment, e.g. your living room, so that there are minimal distractions for your dog. For example, your living room. You cannot expect to teach your dog a new behaviour in the middle of the park when all they want to do is play with their friends or go sniffing for a squirrel.

Once your dog understands a behaviour then you can begin to increase the 3Ds:

- Distance
- Distraction
- Duration

I will go into the 3Ds further on.

To really build value and understanding in a behaviour you must start to increase the 3Ds.

For example:

Can your dog sit 5 meters away from you while you bounce a ball?
Can your dog lie down 3 meters away from you while you dance around singing?
Can your dog recall while you throw a ball in the opposite direction?
Can your dog respond to their name while they hear someone opening the biscuit tin?

Always adjusting the 3Ds of a behaviour means that no matter how good/embedded you think a behaviour is, it can always be improved.

You need to remember to change things slowly, do not expect your dog to do an amazing sit in the living room and then expect them to do it in the middle of a busy beach.

Build value in doing behaviours in all sorts of environments with all sorts of distractions - this is called **proofing,** but just think about it as a difficulty level. Put the 3Ds together and they are the overall difficulty of a behaviour you are teaching.

So not matter what you are teaching your dog, you need to start simply so they cannot fail, then gradually increase the 3Ds to build a strong and valuable behaviour.

No matter how well you think you have trained your dog's behaviour, it can always be improved by increasing the 3Ds.

Part 1

Where it all began

Many years ago, when I made the decision to get my first dog, I realised that I'd spent a lot of time around many other animals and could easily take care of them, but I didn't have the first idea how to look after a dog. I knew that I would need to feed, walk and love it, but I didn't have the first clue about training.

Before I jumped feet first into my puppy hunt, I researched breeds and I narrowed my choice down to three breeds.

1.   Weimaraner
2.   Chinese Crested
3.   Labrador

Those that have been around me for years will know that my final decision was a Labrador, but I wanted a golden dog (funnily enough two of my current dogs are part Chinese Crested).

It took weeks and weeks of hunting to find a golden dog, then I swear I had a dream to check the Horse and Hound magazine. I headed off to buy the magazine and I couldn't believe it, there was a golden dog available less than a ten-minute drive from my home.

It was a sign and Max came home.

From that moment on, I was OBSESSED! In a good way of course, I could not get enough of learning more and more about dog training and behaviour. For years Max taught me more than I could have imagined. But what I never really learnt was anything about problem behaviours, as Max was a complete and total angel. He didn't have a bad bone in his body, I think the naughtiest thing he ever did was run off with the cooked chicken from the BBQ - I couldn't blame him for that, it was within his reach.

As Max aged I wanted to add another dog to the family, and another serendipitous moment came along when I happened to connect with an old school friend who had this one little black fluffy mutt left - "White Tip!" At the time it was coming up to Valentine's Day and I'd asked my boyfriend to get me these awful shoes, which he refused to get! I am thrilled he refused because I wouldn't have been compelled to send him a picture of the black fluffball saying I'd chosen a different Valentine's present. I got a text back… "Oh Sh*t!" Without a doubt, Dexter was a much better choice than shoes and he learnt all he knows from the best dog there was, Max.

The difference between a Labrador and a mixed breed of terrier and lapdog was apparent, I needed to learn even more! Oh, so very much more! Dexter has taken me on the wildest journey of them all (so far) from the Sussex countryside to the main ring at Crufts.

This is where my barking mad journey began, with the addition of terriers. Of course, Max would bark, but not even close to the amount the terriers do.

This was the catalyst for me increasing my behavioural and training knowledge and, I have since learnt, that I will never stop learning. There are new scientific studies all the time providing us with more evidence regarding behaviour; we can only get better at communicating with our dogs, and our other animals too.

Bark Identification

A lot of what you are going to do will require you to be calm and relaxed, shouting at your dog while they are barking will only encourage them to bark more as they think you are joining in, which will only encourage the barking further. Shouting (joining in) is attention as far as your dog is concerned and they will work to maintain that attention because they like it.

Therefore, to begin with I would like you to sit down with a cuppa and have a think about your dog's barking.

First you need to establish what type of barking your dog is doing as well as when and where.

Once you can identify these triggers, you can work on the tricks and tools to resolve the problem. You may need to watch your dog carefully to be certain what sort of barking they do or you may know straight away from reading the following descriptions.

7 most common reasons a dog will bark:

Alarm Barking: A response to noises and sights etc.
Attention-Seeking Barking: Used as an attempt to get your attention for some reason.
Compulsive Barking: Barking for no apparent reason accompanied with a repetitive movement.
Frustration-Induced Barking: Due to confinement, boredom, or separation.
Greeting Barking: Barking to say "hello".
Socially Facilitated Barking: Responding to another dog's bark.
Territorial Barking: People, dogs, or other animals near their territory.

For example, this is why my dogs bark:
Dexter – Barks as a greeting and territorial when outside and people are passing the house.
Cassi – Barks out of frustration when she wants something she cannot get, greeting, social barks at others and territorial when outside and others are passing.
Beanz – Barks as an alarm to any unexpected noise inside or outside the

house, attention seeks, frustrated at separation, and territorially barks (this is part of his breed's traits which you will also need to take into account with your dog).

Alan – Barks for attention, frustration and territorial.

Just because I am a dog trainer does not mean that I have perfect pooches.

Using the table on the following pages detail which type of bark you recognise. You may recognise more than one (which is quite likely) - if so, make a list starting with the type you find most frustrating and work down to the least frustrating. The most frustrating one is what you are going to work on first. All the barking will be linked and the same skills will be used to tackle all of them. However, working on the toughest one first will enable you to feel confident and e quipped to deal with getting to the easier ones later - you may find that less frustrating barking begins to reduce without you even specifically working on it.

If you have more than one dog, complete a separate table for each dog. You can use this program in a multidog household, but it is likely that training will need to be done separately to ensure that there is a clear understanding from each dog.

Fill out as many details as possible, such as:

In what area of the home does the barking occur? Is it at any particular time of day? Are there any similarities or patterns that you can pinpoint with the barking? Is it when your dog sees or hears anything in particular? Detail as much information as you can as this will help you to understand more about what is going on.

		Details
1	Alarm Barking	
2	Attention-Seeking Barking	
3	Compulsive Barking	

4	Frustration-Induced Barking	
5	Greeting Barking	
6	Socially Facilitated Barking	
7	Territorial Barking	

How did you get on?
Were you easily able to recognise your dogs barking?
Were there some instances that you have not considered before?
Has reviewing the barking helped you to see a pattern?
Have you been able to establish where you will start?

If you still have some work to do you can use the timetable at the back of this book to note down any barking, why it happened and in what location and then identify it using the seven options and note that too.

Now you have a better understanding of the issue, you should be able to answer these questions:

1. What is causing your dog to bark?
2. Which location is the most problematic?
3. What type of bark is your dog doing?

Using this knowledge, you can begin to work out how best to encourage more suitable behaviours that you want to see.

Control and Management

Now you have identified your most problematic barking issue I would like you to examine it. One of the easiest things you can look into is restricting visual access around areas that may be causing the excessive barking.

For example, I have got sticky film covering my living room window and I have blocked the holes in my garden wall that they like to look out of. I have also invested in some fake plastic birds to discourage the larger birds from landing in the garden. This way I have been able to control what my dogs can see so they are no longer prompted by visual stimulus to bark.

In practise if a dog keeps barking at a dustbin, the easiest thing to begin with is to remove the dustbin. Therefore, it will help if we can remove some visual triggers that impact your dog's barking habit, do not worry these items can be added back in later.

Most of the training that you will be doing will be in areas that you can control and manage, this allows you to set your dog up to succeed in a situation - if your dog can succeed, you will begin to build a stronger understanding that there is more value in doing a behaviour other than barking. If your dog can bark at whatever it is that is causing them to bark, this continues because they find some level of reward in the barking. **Dog is rewarded for barking = continued barking.** We will look at what your dog finds rewarding later in the book.

By setting our dogs up to succeed they are less likely to be able to practise the unwanted behaviour. Therefore, if your dog is in a situation where you know they historically bark, stay with them and work with them to encourage alternative and more desirable behaviours in that situation.

If your dog practises an unwanted behaviour, then it will take longer to resolve. We want to ensure they get NO reinforcement for unwanted behaviours, but that they get a huge amount of reinforcement and reward for a more desirable behaviour.

Basic Behaviours

Now it is time to start looking at your dog's basic behaviours.

Sit - Down - Recall - Reflex to Name - Hand Touch

If you are not sure what all these behaviours are, you can find details of how to teach them at the back of the book in appendix A – Teaching your dog how to…

On the next page you will find a table of behaviours and locations. I would like you to think about how well your dog knows each of these behaviours and rate them accordingly between one and five - one being the behaviour is unlikely to happen, five being the behaviour will happen.

Do not worry if your dog cannot do all these behaviours, or if a behaviour they can do is not listed, you can add your own in the spaces provided. Answer honestly, it is only you will see them and you will need to refer to them later.

The aim of this exercise is to help you realise how reliable behaviours are in certain situations. Working on just one or two of these behaviours to a high level will be a great start to your training, as you can easily keep a track of their progress and not overwhelm yourself or your dog.

For example, I know when I am indoors with my dogs most of the listed behaviours are rated quite highly, but then the scoring starts to decrease for some behaviours when environments start to get more interesting. This is perfectly normal, but it gives you a base line to work from if you know which behaviours can be improved on and in what situations.

Do not try to carry out long training sessions. Short sessions of no more than three minutes are more effective. Your training sessions should be short, fun, and full of energy. This way you can aim to get quick and active responses to any verbal cues. It does not matter if you work on one, two, three or all of them, it is about taking a little bit of time to work on building value and understanding on the basics in as many situations as possible.

Right there!

Just a quick word on teaching your dog new and better behaviours. It really helps if you can make it clear to your dog what it was they did that earned them their reward. You can use a simple word like "yes" or "good" the moment you see your dog do something you would like them to repeat. This way your dog learns that when they have heard this word, a reward (something your dog likes) will follow. This is called **marking** if you would like to use a marker word then read the additional information in Appendix B. It is not essential, but when working at a distance it can be very helpful so I would recommend using a marker word.

	1	2	3	4	5
Sit indoors					
Sit in the garden					
Sit outside the house					
Sit in the park					
Sit in the woods					
Down indoors					
Down in the garden					
Down outside the house					
Down in the park					
Down in the woods					
Recall indoors					
Recall in the garden					
Recall outside the house					
Recall in the park					
Recall in the woods					
Reflex to name indoors					
Reflex to name in the garden					
Reflex to name outside the house					
Reflex to name in the park					
Reflex to name in the woods					
Hand Touch indoors					
Hand Touch in the garden					

Ban the Bark

Hand Touch outside the house					
Hand Touch in the park					
Hand Touch in the woods					

Ban the Bowl

One of the most important things you can do for your dog is to…

… DITCH THE FOOD BOWL.

Your dog's food is one of the most valuable items, so do not give it away for **FREE**.

For as many meals as possible, all food should now be used as a way of training your dog in the above behaviours. Whether that is from their daily food allowance or a few rewards, make them earn their goodies. I would suggest you just ditch the bowl for enrichment reasons alone, feed from a snuffle mat or scatter feed in the garden.

Please note, that if your dog is not motivated by food this does not matter, it is still worth training for their meals. Further through the book we will look at the hierarchy of rewards, this is to help show that if your dog prefers rewards other than food you can use this too.

Remember, there are always ways to improve behaviours and this is what we are going to be working on. Without having value in more suitable behaviours, your dog will only carry out behaviours that THEY find re-warding.

You are the one holding the bowl, now use it in the right way. Your dog's bowl is the same as your pay cheque at the end of each month. You would not work for free, would you? Use your dog's food to teach the behaviours you want to see without overloading on too many rewards and giving away something valuable for free.

Now, those of you that raw feed etc… You can still do it, if you are squeamish this is time to get your rubber gloves on and dig in! My dogs are raw fed and I just dive in now, I use their meals for all sorts of training - I even take it out and about sometimes, I just make sure that I have a raw food reward bag, plenty of wet wipes/sanitiser and off we go. Make it work for you!

Rome was not built in a day, and your dog will not be fixed in a day either. Any trainer or device that claim they can be is only be likely doing more harm than good and the unwanted behaviour is likely to return possibly at a greater level. So, take your time on building strong foundations and understanding; rushing will get you nowhere.

As mentioned at the start of the book, in the section entitled 'IMPORTANT' the 3Ds are vitally important if you want to see improvement in behaviours.

If a behaviour is reinforced it will happen more.

Therefore, we are going to remove the reinforcement and reward your dog is getting from the excessive barking and give them something better to do. Just remember that the longer an unwanted behaviour has been practised for, the longer it will take to break the habit, the same as with humans. I still struggle around cakes - especially around a lemon drizzle!

For example, I personally, cannot break the habit of eating junk food, but I am not being rewarded elsewhere with something better, so I continue the bad habit that I enjoy. If someone said to me for every bag of crisps I do not eat they will give me £5, I may change my mind. If someone said to me, they would give me £100 for not eating a bag of crisps, well that's easy, I'd take the £100. This is what we need to do for your dog, give them something bigger and better to focus on.

The 3Ds are all about improving on current behaviours and no matter how amazing you think your dog can do a behaviour, they can always do it a little better.

The 3Ds

Distance – How far away from you can they be to do the behaviour?
Distraction – Can they do the behaviour while something distracting is going on?
Duration – How long can they carry out the behaviour for?

I mentioned earlier thinking about and doing all these extra areas of training is called "**proofing**", essentially it means that we are working on the behaviour so much that they will be able to do the behaviour no matter what else maybe going on around them.

Training your dog out of a habit is hard work, it takes time, effort, commitment, and consistency. You get out what you put in.

Remember to train little and often as much as possible, doing a solid one-hour training session a day is not the best way. Train in small, bitesize segments, I suggest no more than three minutes at a time - just enough time for the kettle to boil!

Summary

Review everything you have read in part one and ensure that you know exactly what you need to do and when:

- · Bark Identification
  - o Do you know what bark/s your dog does and why?
- Control and Management
  - o What environment/s and situation/s causes the barking?
  - o Have you been able to change the environment/s to prevent barking?
  - o How have you done this?
  - o Is there anything you still need to do?
- Remember that if barking can be practiced, it will continue
- Basic behaviours are your new best friend
  - o They can be practised easily and rewarded heavily
  - o Value in other behaviours is essential
- Ditch the food bowl
  - o Feeding your dog in different ways and using meals for training is more enriching
  - o Using your dog's daily food ration means that you do not need to worry about over feeding your dog

- The 3Ds
  - o Distance
  - o Distraction
  - o Duration

Part 2

It only takes one thing…to learn a lesson.

I was very young, under seven years old, we lived at our old house then. I remember being outside in the cul-de-sac scooting along. At the end of the road was this huge oak tree, it had tarmac all around it, but it was very raised, bumpy and cracked where the roots were growing through.

While I scooted around, I fell and cut my knee (not surprising really) and I took something on board that has stayed with me all my life, and I still say this to myself every time something hurts.

While I cried my Mum said to me – "Does it sting?"

I replied through tears that it did indeed sting.

My Mum said – "Stinging means it is getting better!"

I suppose this is true to a certain extent, but I still think that really it's as bad as telling kids that when the ice-cream man plays his tune, it means he has sold out of ice-cream!

However, just that one event, that one sentence has stayed with me all this time, and I still live by it. If something stings, it will get better! Whether that is physical or emotional pain, it will get better.

The reason I've added this story into my book, is to highlight that it can take just one experience to have a lasting impact.

The same applies to your dog and their behaviours, it only takes one experience and the subsequent consequence for something to stick.

Therefore, thinking about why your dog maybe doing something is vital when it comes to behaviour modification. Why does your dog do something? What are they getting out of doing it? Have they historically received reinforcement for doing it? It just takes one time to learn something and the rest of the time to continue reinforcing it.

Don't you just hate those days when everything seems to go wrong! No matter what you try to do, even simple things like making a cup of coffee end in disaster! Your dog has those days too! Just because they don't spill their coffee or burn their toast your dog can have bad days too. Imagine if I was trying to teach you something new when your head just wasn't in the right frame of mind. You are not going to take that information on board as well as you would if you were in the right frame of mind. This leads me on to thresholds and triggers.

Thresholds

Threshold is the fancy word for the point at which you are at your maximum level, it is your personal line in the sand.

Everyone has a different line (threshold), and it varies on how long or how quickly it takes to reach it.

How do you even reach a threshold? On the magical carpet ride that are **triggers.** Triggers cause you to respond to something in a certain way. Jaffa cakes good, spiders bad!

Why on earth are my triggers and the length of my line relevant to stopping my dogs excessive barking? Well, your dog has their own threshold!

Triggers for me are, jaffa cakes good, spiders bad. But too many jaffa cakes will make me feel full, sluggish and in need of a nap. A sudden hairy eight-legged arachnid running across my living room floor will have me screaming and bouncing off the wall. Which of these scenarios is under and over threshold? Well it does not really matter, because whether you are under or over threshold, you are not in the best frame of mind to be taking on any new information.

It is therefore vital to know how your dog is feeling, because if your dog is **OVER** or **UNDER** their threshold then NO VALID LEARNING CAN TAKE PLACE. Which means training your dog when they are not in the right frame of mine, will not be successful. Try and get me to sit still when there is a spider in the room! The same applies to your dog, if they do not yet have enough value in a behaviour to do it in a certain situation, it is not fair to expect them to do it, especially if they are out of their sweet spot

One final example to help. If you are feeling a little sluggish, you have had a few bad nights sleep. You are going to be feeling tired and washed out. You are **UNDER** threshold, if someone decided to teach you advanced physics you won't take it on-board because you are not feeling at your best. The same applies to being **OVER** threshold, there is no point at all trying to teach me anything at a Take That concert, I am so far over threshold that the only thing I am taking in right now is the lads on stage.

What can you do if you know thresholds have been crossed? Calming activities only. This applies to both you and your dog. Relax with a book, take a bubble bath, anything that will help to bring you back to the sweet spot. For your dog some sniffing, a food filled toy for licking, a gentle walk. Nothing too complicated or arousing for either of you until you are feeling more balanced.

To have the most successful training session you need to work in that lovely little cosy **sweet spot** which can be found in between the over and under threshold lines. Thresholds apply to YOU and your DOG, if you are under threshold and your dog is over threshold, how will that work out? What if you and your dog are both over threshold? That is not good! Make sure that training is carried out when you are both in the right frame of mind to avoid frustration and failure.

Recognising thresholds for both you and your dog is just as important as keeping the 3Ds at the forefront of your mind. If your dog is over or under threshold, it does not matter how much you reduce one of the 3Ds your training session will not be as successful as you had hoped.

Triggers

Triggers can be good and bad, they vary for every dog, this is where it is great to be your dog's guru. If you know what triggers push your dog in what direction you will start to recognise how your dog may be feeling and whether you need to do something before their threshold line is crossed.

Examples could be:

Good	Bad
Opening the cupboard where the treats are kept	The doorbell ringing
Taking the lead off the hook	Cat sitting on the garden fence
Opening the toy box	Person walking past a window
Driving into the car park for a woodland walk	A dog barking outside the house
Favourite auntie comes to visit	The window cleaner has arrived

You could even stop some of the bad triggers from happening to help keep your dog in their sweet spot.

For example:

Disable the doorbell (even changing its tone can help sometimes)
Put a sign up to say leave parcels by the front door
Use a cat deterrent to keep that menacing moggie off the fence
Put sticky film across the windows to block the view but still let in the light
Close the curtains when the window cleaner is there

Hopefully, these examples give you an idea of which triggers could be affecting your dog, and therefore the reason/s why they may be barking so much.

So, what happens if someone walks past the window, with a barking dog, the doorbell goes, the neighbour's cat walks through the back garden and then a van door is slammed all in the space of a few minutes? Let me tell you a story about Trigger Stacking.

Trigger Stacking

Once upon a time there was a girl called Jo. One night , she went to bed early because she had a particularly important appointment the following day and she wanted to be well rested for it. Unfortunately, a night of tossing and turning blighted Jo's rest. Fortunately, an hour before her alarm was due. Jo finally drifted off to sleep.

Typically, a power cut occurred in this hour which meant that Jo's alarm didn't go off! Meaning she was going to be late for her appointment if she did not get a wiggle on, she had just enough time for a quick shower. Aarrrrgh! No hot water and a very cold shock to Jo's system. Not to worry, she thought a coffee will warm me up. Oh no! The dog jumped up her with muddy paws from the garden, causing the coffee to spill down her nice top. A quick change into a back-up outfit (as Jo was no stranger to Mr Sod and his laws) and she dashed to the car. GREAT! A flat battery and no taxis available. She dashed straight to the bus stop! Oh, no purse!... I don't need to type the next bit, I think you get where this story is going, all those triggers stacked up and Jo was at breaking point and ready to scream, Jo was **over** threshold.

The same happens to your dog if too many triggers happen in close succession.

Just imagine your dog is resting comfortably in the living room on the back of the sofa, the prime spot to see everything that is going on in their world, with the added advantage of a particularly good view of the treat cupboard in the kitchen.

Then something happens to spoil your dog's wonderful contentment in their emotional **sweet spot.** That noisy dog from down the road is dragging their human past, barking with excitement, to get to the park! That is not fair, your dog wants to go outside and join in! Just as your dog settles down and returns to their lookout, a delivery man appears in a bright jacket and rings the doorbell then knocks loudly causing a right commotion. You go and collect the package of dog stuff you have purchased, as you need to hide it before the other half sees. Your dog now wants to go out in the garden to investigate the smell of the visitor, but before they can inhale the smells from under the gate your dog sees next door's cat is sitting on the fence giving it the whole "Ha ha ha! You can't get me up here!". Well, your dog could now be **over** threshold. That training session you had planned in five minutes time, forget it.

Hopefully these two scenarios helped to explain trigger stacking, it is just one thing after another to unbalance you from your personal **sweet spot.**

When a dog goes over threshold no real learning takes place, there is no point in asking them to sit etc. If you had missed a meeting because of the first scenario the last thing you would want to do is listen to someone asking you to do stuff. The best thing we can do for both us and our dogs is create some calm to prevent any more triggers building up.

I've created a little infographic to help as well, but I think that this is enough for you to realise that sometimes you just need to pop your pup to bed with a lovely Kong and a belly scratch, until they come back down to earth. Recovery time does vary by dog, so another reason why you need to become your dog's guru.

Your Trigger Task

List your dog's triggers and give each one a score out of five, one being least arousing, five being most arousing.

For example:

Doorbell – 3
Bird – 1
Cyclist – 2
Another dog barking – 4

If, in the space of a morning, your dog experiences:
Doorbell + two birds + a dog barking = 9

What if your dog's threshold line is ten? One more trigger could be enough to push them over threshold, it is your job to take steps now and avoid more triggers.

Try working around each trigger (gradually), using the 3Ds again, but reducing them so your dog is far enough away (**distance)** from the trigger to be able to offer you a behaviour you were expecting. That could be at the far end of the living room when they see a cyclist go past. It might be that you need to close one curtain so that your dog's view is slightly restricted (**dis-**

traction). Only train for a short period of time so that your dog does not become too frustrated or encounter too many triggers **(duration).**

The trick is building new associations with these triggers, this will help to reduce your dog's arousal around them, which means better training will follow. Better training means better behaviours. Everything is linked, therefore it is VITAL to be aware of how aroused your dog is and what it is that has caused the arousal.

Below is a graph showing how triggers could stack up for your dog.

Trigger Stacking

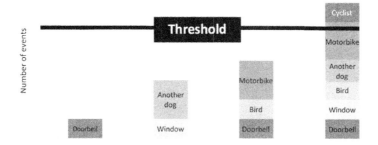

How triggers can stack up

IMPORTANT SUMMARY

Being able to understand more about thresholds, triggers and trigger stacking is vital because it will help you to realise why your dog may be doing something, and why it is your dog could do a behaviour yesterday, but not today.

Triggers have different values, so your dog may see/hear/smell three small triggers or one big trigger which will put them over threshold.

Your dog may see a bird on the lawn searching for worms, but this may not be as arousing as a child riding their scooter outside the front window.

If you learn your dogs triggers and how arousing each one is, it will help your training sessions be more successful.

You do not need to remember the jargon words, what you need to remember is how single and multiple events can affect you and your dog.

Teaching speak and settle

"Speak! But I want my dog to STOP barking!"

Yes, I hear you, but one of the easiest ways to start reducing barking is by putting a bark on cue! Counter intuitive I know, but we now need your dog to bark so you can reinforce, reward, and put it on cue!

From this point forward you must now ensure that unless you have asked for your dog to bark it must **NOT** be rewarded/reinforced.

Do not leave your dog unattended in situations and environments where you know that they have a history of barking – not only will this allow them to practise the behaviour, it is also a missed opportunity to reinforce the behaviour you want to see.

Speak

Encourage your dog to bark, so whether that is with play, excitement, ringing the doorbell etc, we need to get your dog to bark.

When your dog barks you need to **mark** and **reward** this behaviour.

Keep repeating this so your dog begins to understand that it is the bark that is earning the reward.

You can easily add a hand signal, before you encourage your dog to bark, hold your ear lobe (or any other hand signal you may choose). Encourage the bark, mark and reward. Keep working at this until just the hand signal prompts a bark.

Do not add a verbal cue just yet, you do not want to name an inferior behaviour. Once your dog is successfully barking with a hand signal about 90% of the time, add in your verbal cue if you like. Proceed in this order to add a verbal cue:

- Give your verbal cue
- Follow this with the hand signal
- When your dog barks, mark, and reward

If your dog begins to struggle remove the verbal cue and go back to the hand signal. No matter what, you should set your dog up to succeed - you can always go back a step if it is not quite there. Do not keep pushing forward on a behaviour that is not right. You cannot run before you can walk, take your time, strive for progress not perfection and concentrate on building the 3Ds gradually.

Settle

Settle is about encouraging your dog to relax in a certain place, this is immensely helpful both at home and out and about. This is because if you teach your dog to settle on an easy to carry around blanket, you can then teach them to settle anywhere! Whether that is indoors, outdoors, a friend's house, a café; the uses for having a good settle are endless so it is a great behaviour to teach.

Start off with your chosen blanket directly in front of you (make sure it is a suitable size for your dog) and some rewards to hand. As your dog comes over to investigate the rewards you are holding they will interact with the blanket in some way. They may look at it, they may sniff it or they may tread on it straight away. No matter what, as your dog orientates towards you and the blanket, you need to **mark** and drop the **reward** on the blanket.

Then I would like you to say "OK" as a **release word** (if you have already trained another release word, then just use this). The release word is to let your dog know that it is alright to move away from the blanket. As you say your release word, throw another reward a short distance away from you - far enough that your dog must leave the blanket.

As your dog releases from the blanket to eat the reward, just wait; your dog should orientate back towards you and the blanket in the hope of another yummy morsal - as your dog returns to the blanket, **mark** and **reward** again.

What if your dog does not return to you and the blanket? Then it is time to look at your hierarchy of rewards (See Appendix B) and use something else that has a higher value to your dog.

Keep repeating this exercise and gradually your dog will learn that interacting with the blanket is what is earning them their reward. Once you are sure your dog understands that touching the blanket is earning the reward you can start to add a verbal cue if you would like, but it is not essential. When you have released your dog with the "OK" as your dog is returning to you give this behaviour a verbal cue such as "bed", "settle" anything you like. Then they will begin to put it all together:

- Verbal cue blanket
- Get on blanket
- Get rewarded
- Get released

As you progress through this exercise, you can gradually withhold the reward for a moment to see if your dog offers another behaviour on the blanket. For instance, if your dog is stepping on the blanket withhold the reward and your dog may offer you a sit. YAY! This is what we want to see, we want to see that your dog is problem solving, working out how they can earn their reward.

Keep progressing the exercise, we want to encourage your dog into a down position on the blanket without giving them a down command. This is because if you give your down cue, when you **mark** and **reward,** you will be rewarding the down, and not the interaction with the blanket. We want the blanket to have value on its own to understand not to leave the blanket until you release them with the "OK".

Once your dog is returning to the blanket in front of you and offering a down position at least 90% of the time, I would like you to start moving the blanket away from you slightly. Then start to move a little yourself, keep working with the 3Ds, there are lots of things you can do with them and the more you do with them, the stronger the behaviour will become. Remember, bit by bit and if your dog begins to fail go back a step.

It is vital that, as you move through your training journey your dog has a great understanding of **settle,** which is why increasing and varying the 3Ds around this behaviour is vital. This is a great behaviour to have strongly embedded so that if a trigger for their barking occurs your dog can either remain in their settle place or take themselves there in preparation for a reward.

If like me you have a multidog household, work on this one dog at a time and gradually add either more dogs or more triggers, but do not do it all at once from level one to level ten. Mix it all up, so have a larger trigger and less dogs, or more dogs and a lower trigger.

Start raising your game.

Introducing trigger sounds on purpose in a controlled way

Case Study

I was contacted by a client as her terrier would disappear hunting pheasants. It was deeply upsetting as the dog would disappear for a quite a time, but always returning. The client really wanted to resolve this as they did not want their dog to remain on the lead while walking in areas the pheasants frequented.

After discussing the situation with the client, I asked her what caused her dog to start his hunt. To which she replied:

"Oh! He just has to hear their squawk; he does not even have to see them to chase them!"

Therefore, as well as working on recall skills I asked her to play pheasant sounds on the internet. I asked her to play these sounds on the lowest sound when she had some amazing rewards available. As the dog would hear the squawking he was interested, but of course he is indoors (I doubt there are many domesticated pheasants!).

The client was able to condition her dog so that when her dog heard the pheasants squawk it was more valuable to be around her. Putting this together with some recall games meant that the sound for the unwanted behaviour was no longer a trigger to cause her dog to run off.

This is where the internet really helps, you can find all different types of sounds to suit what you may need.

However, not all trigger sounds may be available easily, this is where you can get creative.

- Record the sound yourself on a phone or dictaphone
- Recreate the sound to appear indoors/in the garden in a controlled environment

Some things that I have done to recreate sounds to recondition my dogs are:

- Hanging spare dangly identification tags together near a window/door so that the wind will create the tingle sound (like dogs passing my house)
- Setting my phone notification to be the same as my doorbell
- Asking neighbours to do silly walks outside of my house
- Asking visitors to open and close their car doors a few times when I know they have arrived

When you are ready, start in an area with the least distraction (such as the kitchen or the living room) and play the sound at a low level so your dog does not react to it. Reward your dog for not reacting to the sound. Play the sound again and repeat, as soon as your dog is not responding to the trigger sound, you can then gradually increase the sound, and the 3Ds.

Do not just blast the sound up to 100% for 20 seconds while your dog is sleeping, and you are in the garden. Remember, you must build up everything gradually, so pick one thing to increase at a time.

- Distance (how far you are away from your dog when you play the noise)
- Distraction (what else is going on when you play the noise)
- Duration (how many times do you play the sound before rewarding your dog)
- Volume

Never play a sound so much that it causes your dog to stress and worry, if your dog is particularly sensitive to a sound, put it on the lowest volume you can, muffle the speaker as well and gradually build it up.

The aim of this exercise is to teach our dog that when they hear the noises that cause them to bark, it is far better and more rewarding if they come to us.

Be mindful that if you hear a noise that you react to (such as a fire alarm) it is the same for your dog. Constant over use of the sound is not going to help anyone, so ensure to train in short sessions and do not overdo it. You are trying to build value around YOU when this noise occurs, not teach your dog that you cause the to noise could blast out at them. It is vital that you start in a nice calm environment, then gradually build it up to suit your dog.

This works for so many situations with our dogs, the jargon terms for this are **counter conditioning** and **desensitisation**. It essentially means that we are exposing our dogs to something they normally respond to at a low level and teaching them to react another way to it - gradually building up the level of exposure.

Case Study

To help explain **counter conditioning** and **desensitisation** further I will use my rescue dog as an example.

When I first got her at eighteen months old, she was reactive and fearful of joggers and cyclists. She would bark and jump at them both on and off the lead and scare the living daylights out of the poor people trying to do their exercise.

Her case is a little more complex than unwanted barking as she could have hurt someone, however, in resolving this I used some of the same principles in this book. Counter conditioning and desensitisation were key in being able to help her become the dog she is today.

I taught her that if she saw something that she did not like she could count on me. It took a lot of dedication and a year of 4am walks, but I could gradually expose her to her triggers. Bit by bit the walks would get later in the morning (thank goodness) and we would encounter a die-hard jogger around 430am, then more at 5am and 6am.

Within a few months we had learnt some of the jogger's routes, so I knew where I could be to wait to watch the jogger go by. It got to a stage where we could go for a walk and it would only be the ones that were unexpected that ran silently up behind us that would cause her to bark and lunge (in fairness, I would be the same if someone came up behind me).

However, we carried on and we got to a stage where every time she saw a jogger/cyclist she would turn to me for a reward, she would be reinforced and rewarded for not reacting to the passing exercise enthusiasts.

It took over twelve months, but finally we were able to walk off lead and not worry about fast moving humans.

Overtime she would even stop looking to me for a reward as she would rather continue her sniffing or playing with friends than come back for what were now boring bits of kibble, as I had reduced the rewards over time.

Keep Raising Your Game

Throughout this book I bark on about working on your **basic behaviours**, it is now time to gradually start practising these behaviours closer to your dog's arousal point(s).

The aim is to practise these behaviours in known barking locations and to build even more value in them in an area where they have a learnt history of barking.

This way, by practising these behaviours in these areas, we know that the distraction will be higher for your dog and, gradually, your dog will be able to listen to and comply with, your cues when you give them.

I am sure that you are probably thinking *"Blooming heck Jo, this training is pretty basic"*. Well yes, that is the point, this way your dog and you are going to be much more successful. It is not about just teaching a great sit, it is about using these simple things to build a bigger and better relationship with your dog that brings with it more engagement and desire to do things with you, rather than choosing something to do on their own…which you are probably not going to like as much.

By doing these simple exercises your dog is succeeding more, if they succeed more, they will want more! I am not talking about teaching a sit for eight hours a day, but if you have thirty seconds, use any rewards you have to hand and ask for a sit or two. Little and often will pay off in dividends, which will build a stronger relationship between you and your dog. If your dog is not engaged enough with you, they will ultimately find a way to reinforce and reward themselves, which in this case is barking. You can also use moments when you see your dog sit on their own, tell them "Good dog!", give them a scratch, a biscuit, throw a ball, whatever you happen to have with you. You would much rather have these behaviours than the barking, so reward them.

I am going to mention this AGAIN, so sorry but you **MUST** remember to keep increasing the 3Ds.

You can increase the **distance** by having your dog closer to the point of arousal, while you move further away from your dog. Maybe add in a little

distraction of a noise in the background or increase the **duration** of the behaviour around a low level of the arousal.

Be warned though, do not increase all the 3Ds at once, move one up, move one down; move two up and one down. Gradually increase them in small increments, if you push too much too quickly, you will have no foundational training to fall back on if it goes wrong. Think about it as adding more pieces to a jigsaw puzzle, if you rush things, pieces can fall on the floor and not make it into the bigger picture.

As well as training in the areas which have the highest arousal, use these areas for enrichment activities, play games, scatter feeding, anything your dog enjoys you should do it around this area so that this area can become a site of good things. Your dog will start to think "When will the next game start?" - rather than waiting for a trigger which causes your dog to bark. Do not go straight to the area, work closer to it, otherwise the value will not have been built up for them to realise that barking at the trigger is no longer as interesting as what you are doing.

Because your dog has built their own value in the areas of high arousal, we want to change their association in these areas with new and more desirable behaviours. Therefore, increase the forms of enrichment in these areas, which will help your dog begin to expect something different and more valuable, rather than reverting to their old game of barking. Essentially, if you are keeping their noses and mouths busy with some form of enrichment - scatter feeding, forage mat or any activity both you and your dog enjoy - barking becomes an incompatible behaviour because your dog is engrossed in sniffing and/or chewing something. If you have worked on your settle, put the blanket there and give them a chew or whatever your dog finds desirable and reward them for every decision that they make that is a step closer to what you are aiming for.

Then it is time for you to get a cuppa, relax and watch from a sensible distance, either in sight or just out of sight of your dog. Just let them get on with what it is that they want to do. Just casually keep an eye on them and be ready to reinforce and reward for any good decisions they make for ignoring a trigger.

Another gentle reminder for you: Once you have started to teach "speak" do not let any unrequested barking be rewarded, remember a reward is ANYTHING your dog wants! It is going to be tough, but it can be done with some thought and management. So do not let your dog out in the garden when the school rush is on and there are more people out and about, or when you know that the bin men are due. Yes, of course there will be unexpected things that crop up, that's life, but it is how you handle these situations from now on that will have the lasting effect.

If your dog does find a moment for a bit of barking, wait for a short time when the barking has stopped (no more than five seconds really, as chances are by this point, they have done another behaviour), casually say to your dog "Quiet!", then you can reward. We will do more with "Quiet!" shortly, but what we want your dog to understand is that barking is no longer rewarded by us (so think about how you may have inadvertently rewarded their barking before). This is how we are going to work on resolving your dog's excessive barking habit.

Your dog can talk the talk, but can you walk the walk?

Another great area to focus on with your dog, is their body language.

Learning your dog's body language, so that you know if they are about to bark, can give you the opportunity to introduce a "Quiet!" or "Shhh!" cue. You may have noticed some body language in training sessions. While working through this book have you started to spot ear twitches or head turns? Can you spot when your dog may be about to bark? Are you aware of additional triggers that you did not know about when you first started? Are you becoming your dog's guru?

Watching your dog and learning what their body language is saying is incredibly helpful. Basically because if you learn to spot when your dog is contemplating barking, then you can add in your ""Quiet!" or "Shhh!" cue (any cue that suits you to mean quiet) before they bark. As you give your cue if your dog does not bark but orientates to you…Yup! You have got it! Reward.

Remember, don't tell your dog to "Quiet!" if they are barking just yet, as you'll just associate barking with that cue, so your dog will think that "Quiet!" means bark and you'll end up needing to change your cue.

Therefore, try to get into the habit of casually having one eye on your dog while you are in a variety of situations at home such as:

- Watching the TV
- Cooking a meal
- Reading a book in the garden

- Sitting at a desk working

Then whatever you are doing, try to be aware of those tiresome triggers that have been causing the barking, such as:

- Seeing a delivery van pull up and know a door will slam
- Realise someone is about to walk past the living room window
- Is the postal worker making their way round?
- Is it the school rush and there is a lot of noise outside?

Yes, you will need eyes in the back of your head for the time being, but if you cannot do this for a certain aspect of your day then remember a little **control** and **management** goes a long way.

It can be simple things such as:

- Not allowing your dog access to see outside the front window, either have them in another room, the blinds/curtains closed or my personal favourite is some of the sticky privacy film. This way they cannot see out, but the light can come in.
- Do not allow unattended access in the garden, you never know when that cat will jump up on the fence.
- Close your windows during the school run to reduce some of the noise.

Do not worry, this will not be forever! We're trying to teach your dog a new habit and if they get a chance to practice the old habit, it will be harder to build value in the new behaviour.

For example, if you are trying to lose weight and you work out at the gym for an hour a day, but three times a week you have an indulgent meal. Yes, you may have deserved it from all the hard work, but your weight loss target will be a little further away. It is still there and reachable, it will just take longer to achieve. However, if you do not have the takeaway meals, you stick to a rigid plan, you will reach your target goal quicker. The same applies for your dog, if they can practice a behaviour randomly, it will make that behaviour stronger. If you want to know why this is, see my fruit machine analogy in Appendix B.

Summary

- Thresholds
  - Over threshold
  - Under threshold
  - Can you recognise when your dog is over or under threshold?
  - Do you know what to do if your dog is over or under threshold?

- Triggers
  - Do you know your dog's triggers?
  - Do you know which ones are bigger than others?
  - Do you know what triggers could push your dog over threshold?
  - Can you recognise when trigger stacking reaches the point where your dog can no longer concentrate?
- Teaching "Speak!" – so that unrequested barking is no longer rewarded. If we only reward requested barking, we stop rewarding unwanted barking.

- Teaching "Settle!" – value in being somewhere other than looking for triggers, building value in settling in a certain place or on a certain thing helps to create a calm and relaxed dog.

- Raise your game – utilise other things, such as sounds, to proof your training - practise, practise and more practise. The only thing holding you back from being more creative when you practise is your imagination. Ask family and friends to help and create practise scenarios.

- Keep raising your game – keep the 3Ds at the front of your training, every behaviour can always be better if you adjust the 3Ds
  - Distance
  - Distraction
  - Duration

Part 3

The only guru you need for your dog…is you!

I don't know anything about you, maybe you have had a similar dog training journey to me or maybe you are learning with your first dog. Even though I have been studying dogs for the last couple of decades, doesn't mean that I know everything.

Any dog trainers (whisperers, gurus or fad celebrities) that claim they know it all, are not being truthful. This is because our knowledge is ever expanding. People can certainly become experts their chosen fields, but they will never know it all.

I know this for a fact because years ago wise humans thought that the Earth was flat and scientists thought that atoms were the smallest thing - both of which we now know are wrong.

Things change, we learn more and we adapt what we do to include our new knowledge.

Knowledge is key, knowing things about your dog is vital. Every dog is different, there is no cookie cutter method for training every dog. The same as every human is different, has different things they like and dislike so are dogs.

I know lots about all of my dogs, I know when certain event occur, that one may enjoy it, one may dislike it and others may be indifferent to it.

By knowing these little things about each of my dogs, I can do so much more, and so can you. Spend the time really getting to know your dog, their personal preferences - it will pay off in the long run. Your training sessions will be more productive if you can work them around your dog and what they like.

Become your dog's Guru

So far, since starting this course, you have identified your dog's barking habits. You know what they are barking at, the locations where the barking occurs and whether your dog has just one main bark that is causing you concern, or more and their various triggers.

What you need to do is figure out which bark (if more than one) is frustrating you the MOST.

You should now be constantly working on your basic behaviours around your daily routine and have confidently added in **speak** and **settle.**

I am also hoping that you have been using the timetable provided (Appendix C) to make a note of training sessions or any other noteworthy events from little wins, big wins, even the little oops moments. Making a note of these moments help you to recognise them and avoid making them again in the future. Keeping a note of your training means you can easily adapt further training sessions as necessary. If needed you can download and print copies of helpful documents

from www.pawsitivity.co.uk/downloads

The more you take responsibility for training your dog, the more you will be able to recognise wins and oops moments. At this point, all you can do is improve.

"Strive for progress not perfection"

Knowing and understanding all this information about your dog and your training (becoming your dog's guru) means that you can be confident making adjustments, where needed, to ensure that behaviours are reinforced, rewarded, and improved.

It is helpful to record your training sessions so that you can review them afterwards. Pop the kettle on and record a training session, you can review your training session while you enjoy the well-earned beverage to see if there is anything you missed and make any notes of how to improve during the next session.

Keep the 3Ds in the forefront of your mind, they are the key to everything, you cannot expect your dog to move from level one to level ten without passing through the levels in between. That is just setting them up for failure, which means frustration for your dog and that is just not fair.

Hopefully, you should be at the stage where you can start working on **settle** and **speak** and your basic behaviours around distractions. If you are not sure when some certain distractions will occur, you could ask family and friends or even other dog owners you meet on walks to assist you or use the power of the internet to find some sounds that you know cause your dog to bark. Our aim is for your dog to work around these sounds, not react to them, so it would be advisable to work with these sounds at a low level.

Go back to your original basic behaviours' scores and see whether they have improved or whether they still need some work.

Case Study

While working with my own dogs and their barking I realised that a lot of the time they would hear other dogs passing in the street without me knowing about it. They could hear the other dogs bark and their tags jingling on their collars. There was one dog that would drive my pups into a barking frenzy, the most gorgeous German Shepherd called Dexter.

This was because as Dexter approached my house, he would bark (not surprising if every time he approached he would be subjected to a bunch of unruly terriers telling him to move on).

I asked Dexter's owner if she would be kind enough to message me when she thought she may be passing my house and she was happy to help. This meant that as I knew a trigger was likely to appear, I could prepare for some training with my mouthy mongrels!

I prepped myself with some super yummy rewards (as Dexter is a huge trigger for my mutts). However, I made the mistake of starting off in my back garden and the session was a complete failure, the bark from them all was extreme. Yes, I expected too much of them, it was my fault I just went from level one to level ten with nothing in between.

I beat myself up for making such a silly mistake (I am only human after all), but did I do it again? No. I was more prepared.

The next time I only went out with two of my dogs and to the furthest part of my garden. I gradually built it up with more dogs and getting closer.

The progress was surprisingly quick after that, in two weeks I could sit right by where the dogs could see Dexter pass and they decided that barking at him was not worth it.

Not it does still need work of course, I cannot always be in the garden and ready for when these triggers pass, but we are well on the road to improvement.

The final three

If you have made it through the book this far, your dog should have at least one basic behaviour that is better than all the rest, whether that is a sit or a down, it does not matter, I just want you to be able to recognise which one it is. Which is the basic behaviour that you know you can count on? (write it in below)

I can rely on my dog to............... no matter what distraction is around.

My dogs have a mixture of sits and downs that they are stronger with, which is fine, I don't mind at all so long as they do the behaviour I ask for. The other behaviours that are not so reliable can be worked on further by amending the **distance, distraction,** and **duration (3Ds)**.

So, what is the final three? These are the final three behaviours that you should add to your dog's repertoire.

There is no rush for these, but they certainly do have a place in your training toolbox. I have listed them in the order you should work through them:

1. Quiet
2. Hand Touch
3. Eye Contact

Some of these behaviours you may already have, in which case fantastic, just work on those 3Ds so that they can become behaviours you can rely on around a variety of triggers.

The reasons I would like you to teach these behaviours:

Quiet – Well that is a no brainer, we want our dog to be quiet
Hand Touch – Teaching our dog that pressing their nose to our hand is valuable, it creates an easy to see focal point and having a place to run to and touch brings them away from an arousal area.
Eye Contact – Similar to the hand touch but this can be done at a further distance away to get our dogs attention so we can give them an additional cue such as a down or a recall.

See the individual training guides at the end of the book in **appendix A**

Time to get paws-itive

I have left the best until last, yes this is my last chocolate and I'm giving it to you.

This final behaviour that you are going to teach your dog is called a **positive interrupter** or my *get out of jail free card*.

Your positive interrupter is going to be used when you suddenly realise that your dog is about to do something that you would rather they did not. For example, you may spot a cat is walking across the garden and your dog has looked up, spotted the cat and is about to start world war three on this poor moggy.

You can use your positive interrupter to basically interrupt your dog's train of thought and get them out of Dodge!

Positive Interrupter

A **Positive Interrupter** needs to be taught like anything else, so when your dog hears it, they know an *amazing* thing is about to happen. This should be your ULTIMATE puppy party sound so when your dog hears you say it, they will stop whatever it is they were thinking of doing and come straight to you where the good stuff is.

Look back at your dog's personal reward list, everything on this list can be used with your positive interrupter. There should be some food, toys, interaction from you with games or fussing. When I use my positive interrupter with my dogs, I go all out and use as many things as possible that I have available, but no matter what I have around, I always have plenty of hugs and bum scratches to go around.

Your **positive interrupter** is not a cue such as sit, come, down, it should be a fun sound or phrase that is distinguishable from anything else that you may say so that when they hear it, all they can think about is stopping whatever it is they are doing and to get to you as quickly as possible.

For example, if you need to get my attention then play a song by *Take That*. If I hear a Take That song, that is it! I stop what I am doing, and I am off in

Jo-land living my best life! Seriously, I worked in an office once and if the song *"Never Forget"* came on the radio, I was up, dancing around the office and encouraging others to participate in the iconic hand clapping. Yes, completely bonkers, but that is how you get me to stop whatever it is I am doing.

So, what gets your dog's paws clapping, ears pricking and tails wagging?

Sadly, as much as I tried, the sound of the TT boys was not enough to get my dogs attention (even though they love it when I am dancing around my living room). To get my dogs attention I have trained them with a **positive interrupter** of "Pup-pup-pup-pup-pup-pup".

You do not want to use your dog's name for this because you use your dog's name a LOT during each day and don't reward -therefore our dogs names become devalued (Just look at my dog Beanz as a prime example of this). I also have a lot of dogs, so I need the sound to mean something to ALL my dogs at once. I know that if one of them is up to mischief, the others will not be far behind!

Decide on what you would like to use as your **positive interrupter** it can be anything, so long as it is easy for you to call out when you need it most.

Here are some examples of **positive interrupters** I have heard over the years.

Yipee-yipee-yipee
Duck-duck-duck-duck
Whizz-whizz-whizz-whizz
Beep-beep-beep-beep

You cannot use something that cannot easily be heard, such as clicking your tongue. If you are outside and the wind is blowing and the cows are moo-ing, will your dog hear it? If the answer is no, then you cannot use it.

Once you have chosen your **positive interrupter** start in a quiet environment with your dog in front of you.

Make your chosen noise, drop a reward, throw a toy, give out hugs and love and have a PUPPY PARTY. *Never forget:* This noise should not be overused and you should always have AMAZING fun with your dog when you use it.

Train your **positive interrupter** the same as every other behaviour, build those 3Ds gradually. Your aim is for this noise to be your dog's version of my *Take That* effect.

Perfect this cue and you will soon be dancing around and clapping yourself at how effective it can be!

3Ds Challenge

You have heard me mention the 3Ds enough now to probably make you hate the phrase! In all seriousness these are what are going to get you through any problem behaviour, as well as building a strong understanding in behaviours that you do want.

I now challenge you to the following:

- Dog sits while you are 5 meters away indoors
- Dog sits while you are 10 meters away indoors
- Dog sits while you are out of sight indoors (make sure you can see them somehow)
- Dog sits while you are 5 meters away outdoors
- Dog sits while you are 10 meters away outdoors
- Dog sits while you are out of sight outdoors (make sure you can see them somehow)
- Dog lies down while you are 5 meters away indoors
- Dog lies down while you are 10 meters away indoors
- Dog lies down while you are out of sight indoors (make sure you can see them somehow)
- Dog lies down while you are 5 meters away outdoors
- Dog lies down while you are 10 meters away outdoors
- Dog lies down while you are out of sight outdoors (make sure you can see them somehow)
- Dog speaks while you are 5 meters away indoors
- Dog speaks while you are 10 meters away indoors
- Dog speaks while you are out of sight indoors (make sure you can see them somehow)
- Dog speaks while you are 5 meters away outdoors
- Dog speaks while you are 10 meters away outdoors
- Dog speaks while you are out of sight outdoors (make sure you can see them somehow)
- Dog runs to you from 5 meters away and does a hand touch
- Dog runs to you from 10 meters away and does a hand touch
- Dog runs to you from out of sight and does a hand touch

How did you do?

These are literally just some things to have a play with; the opportunities to train and progress with every behaviour are endless, you just need to take the time to do it and *strive for progress not perfection.*

Building habits which last a lifetime

Throughout the book I hope that you have been building your understanding of your dog's behaviour and how you can successfully modify areas that you would like to change when it comes to their excessive barking.

You should now have a good understanding of your dog's personal strengths and weaknesses as well as your own.

You have learnt that the most simple and basic behaviours can be used to great advantage to help you in your quest to banning the bark.

With all the things you have learnt, it is now time to start consciously bringing everything together. You may not have realised that you have been doing this anyway, but just by thinking about how you can **control** and **manage** your dog's environment and situations they find themselves in, you are able to set your dog up to **succeed**.

Here we go, I am going to say it again, I want you to make a plan of attack.

Since you first started this book things could have changed.

To start with what was your biggest problem.
Has this now reduced?
Have you now noticed another problem area?

No matter what, you and your will dog grow and change together. Your relationship evolves all the time and things that were once important may no longer even be on your radar.

Think about what needs the most work, as this will now be your next area to focus on, make a training plan for the next day/week/month.

This way you can watch the progress, you can put plans into place for how to deal with situations as they arise. I want you to be certain you know what level your dog is at so that you do not set them up to fail.

Do you know what now triggers your dog to bark?
Do you know what rewards your dog likes best?

Can you ask others to help you in training your dog so that you can increase the 3Ds?

It is all very well and good me telling you to teach all these basic behaviours, but what is the good of it if your dog cannot **settle** when someone is at the door or give you a **hand touch** as the noisy neighbourhood dog goes past.

All those things you have been working on with your dog over the past few weeks - it is now time to see how far you have really come.

I would like you to pick your strongest basic behaviour and see if your dog can do this behaviour when their trigger occurs, can they settle? Can they be quiet? Can they sit?

You may still be in the same room as your dog when you are training, this is fine, you will gradually be able to increase that **distance** so that you can be in another room when a trigger occurs.

Your aim is to build value in more desirable behaviours that will last a lifetime.

Keep in mind that if a behaviour has been practiced for some time, it is going to take longer to teach a new behaviour.

If things start to wobble then go back a step or two, do not continue to push forwards until you are sure that your dog has reached a certain level of understanding.

Maintaining the behaviours you want

If there is a particular behaviour your dog does that you are thrilled with, and you do not want the previous undesirable behaviour to return you should occasionally reward your dog to keep this behaviour valuable and strong! Remember, rewarding randomly is especially important because you are using the **fruit machine** for your OWN gain Winner! Winner!

Everything needs a little maintenance to keep it running smoothly, like your vehicle, your home, yourself.... whatever! When a behaviour you like is being achieved 90% of the time, you can start moving training sessions further apart and reduce the value of the rewards as well as rewarding less frequently, do this gradually though! You do not want to ruin all your hard work.

One of the most important things to remember is that you get out what you put in. If you suddenly stop your training, which behaviour will your dog do? Which one is most valuable for them?

Should behaviours start to slip, you need to take a step back, get your guru back on and figure out what is going on and where things can be adjusted to bring back your dog's desire to start the game with you again. Whether that is using a more valuable treat or rewarding more often this will vary depending on your dog. Of course, it is worth thinking about how frequently your dog is getting the same reward, are they getting bored with it? I love my jaffa cakes, but there are only so many I will eat before turning away from them.

Build everything up slowly, *strive for progress* and, if it goes wrong, just go back a step.

No matter what, you are in this for the long haul to change a behaviour that you find frustrating and annoying. These sorts of changes do not happen overnight. They take time, dedication, consistency and understanding.

So long as you work in small incremental stages and do not rush ahead before your dog is ready, you will start to see progress. When you do, it will motivated you to keep going until you have built some great new behaviours that you can pat yourself on the back for.

Good luck on your journey, now go and Ban that Bark!

Summary

- Become your dog's guru – learn all about your dog, what they like, what they dislike. The more you get to know about your dog, the more successful your training will be.
- "Quiet!" – Teaching your dog that being quiet is more valuable than barking is one of the final tools you will need, so that even if any unwanted barking does occur, you will be equipped to stop it quickly and it won't continue and build into a theatrical finale.
- Hand Touch – Builds focus on your hand to prevent looking for triggers, if your dog is looking for something to bark at, bring them back to focus on you with a simple wave of your hand. Your hand waving means that something good will follow, so why bother looking out of the window to bark at the passer by.
- Eye Contact – Builds value and focus on you, if your dog is always ready and waiting for the next game with you, they will have no need to make their own game.
- Positive Interrupter – to influence your dog's train of thought before they do something unwanted, this can be used in more situations than you can imagine, this is your 'get out of jail free' card. Use this as your "pull in case of emergency", you'll be ready for any sudden change.
- 3Ds challenge – proofing, proofing and more proofing of the 3Ds – only your imagination is going to limit you. See how far you can build it, changing these will keep it fresh and interesting for you and your dog. If you or your dog are bored of a behaviour, then why are you doing it?
- Consistency to build the habits of a lifetime – You and anyone that spends time with your dog must be consistent. It is the same as any good habit you wish to continue in life. I find it VERY hard to walk past the aisle with the Jaffa Cakes in, and yes sometimes I slip, but I get straight back on the wagon and move on from that one wobble rather than allow it to derail me. We're human, we're not infallible, you can get right back to training even when blips happen.

APPENDIX A

How to teach your dog…

Lie Down
Eye contact
Hand touch
Sit
Quiet
Recall
Reflex to name

Lie Down

I like to teach down with two methods:

Capturing – Reward your dog when you see them choosing to lie down, mark and reward, simple as that.

Lure – With your dog in a sit and a reward in your hand, place the reward in front of your dogs' nose and slowly move your hand to the ground. As you start to see your dog bending down from their front legs, give them the reward and repeat. Each time see if your dog will move a little further down until they are in the down position.

Once your dog is freely offering a down position for a reward then you can start adding a verbal cue - do not add a verbal cue too soon as you will be naming an incomplete behaviour.

Eye Contact

Why is this a great exercise to teach? Well, if your dog is not looking at you, they are certainly not listening to you. We want our dogs to be looking at us wondering when the next lovely thing is going to happen.

With a handful of rewards and your dog in front of you, drop a reward, then another, then another, then another, then another…do you see where I am going with this? Then stop dropping rewards, your dog will wonder why the lovely reward rain has stopped and will look up into the sky…or your eyes and when they look at you, drop another reward. Simple as that, repeat until your dog understands that looking at you means it rains more rewards.

Do not practice this exercise if your dog is uncomfortable with eye contact, concentrate on a hand touch instead.

Hand Touch

The hand touch is a great exercise to teach your dog. You can use it to focus them and even to assist with recall.

First place a reward between your middle and ring finger, this is to help guide your dog to your hand and build value in touching your hand. Keep the reward here, do not let your dog have this piece!

As your dog investigates the reward between your fingers, as their nose touches your hand, mark and give a reward from the other hand. Continue to repeat this by putting your hand back in front of your dog again, and mark and reward as he investigates again. You may only need to do this ten times before your dog gets the idea of the game.

Once your dog is happily touching your hand with his nose you can try removing the reward from between your fingers. However, if your dog stops touching your hand put the reward back to tempt them to touch your hand again. It is vital to remember that should your dog fail, go back to the previously successful point.

Use both hands as the nose touch hand, do not always have your dog touching the same hand, mix it up a bit to keep it different.

Once your dog has really built value in the hand touch, you can start using it outside in other areas and proofing the value in your hand. You can even add it to your recall so that your dog can see the hand high in the air and then you can bring it down for them to touch as they get closer to you. Just keep increasing the 3Ds.

Recall

Start by teaching eye contact, reflex to name, also hand touch is brilliant to use with recall as this can be used as a visual recall as your dog will see your hand from a distance and want to get back to touch it to earn their reward.

Tennis

Play "tennis" with your dog, start indoors and then the garden with another human (you can build up even more humans if you want, just so long as you know who is going to call your dog next so there is no confusion). Recall your dog between you and keep the "tennis" game full of energy and fun.

As your dog starts to run to you, you could walk backwards and adding in some additional movement and fun.

Your dog will soon learn the tennis pattern and run between each of you without someone recalling him, well that is not learning to recall, that is learning to run between people for food. When your dog starts to run to someone that has not called him, someone else should call your dog to ensure that the recall is being listened to, and not the pattern being learnt.

Hide and Seek

Play "hide and seek" with your dog, start indoors and in the garden. If it is with one person drop a small pile of treats to keep your dog busy while you dash somewhere out of sight, if there is more than one person then when your dog is going to find one of you, the other can hide somewhere else. Keep it VERY easy to begin with and gradually make it harder as your dog understands the game. If your dog starts to struggle then just make it easier again as you do not want any frustration or boredom coming in to make finding you less exciting. When your dog finds you, have a pup-party, go crazy, food, toys, scratches, the lot.

Chuck and Run

A fast and fun game to play is "chuck and run", this is all about playing and chasing. Throw a reward in the opposite direction to you for your dog to get, as your dog goes to get it go in another direction at any speed you wish, stay in sight this time though as it is not hide and seek. As your dog orientates to you wondering what on earth you are doing, give a call and keep going. As your dog catches you up have a pup-party.

Going into the big wide world

When you take your recall game out into the open for the first time your dog should be in a harness and on long line, never attach a long line to a collar as if it were to get caught then a sudden pull on your dog's neck could cause an injury. Make sure you have some super yummy food and exciting toys as well.

Start in a quite environment, there is no point starting in the middle of a busy park as that is setting your dog up to fail and that is not fair.

Reflex to name

This is teaching your dog that when they hear their name, they automatically look around to where it came from.

With your dog in front of you say their name and then drop a reward and repeat.

It does not matter what your dog is doing at the time as you are not rewarding a behaviour, you are conditioning them to realise that when they hear their name something nice happens.

Keep this exercise fun and entertaining but remember that if you use their name too much without a reward it will become less valuable.

Think about the number of times you may use your dog's name and the context. For example, if you use their name when they have done something you would prefer that they had not done, then this will also devalue their name as it will not have a positive association.

Think about giving your dog a pet name. Yes, a pet name for your pet it sounds odd. However, if you have another name such as "Pickle" "Cheeky" "Trouble" "Squirt", these are additional words that you can use without devaluing their name for when you really need it. For example, when you want to try and stop them rolling in something disgusting.

Sit

With your dog in front of you and a reward in your hand, place the reward on your dogs' nose and very slowly raise your hand upwards.

As the weight starts to shift to your dog's bottom, mark, and reward. Continue like this in small incremental steps until their bottom is on the floor. When your dog is in the sit position, give them a few more rewards while they remain in this position.

When your dog is consistently following your hand into the sit position try removing the reward from your hand but still use the same hand movement. If your dog sits, then mark and reward from the other hand.

If this is working, start adding the verbal cue before the hand signal. Before you know it your dog will be sitting on the verbal cue to get the reward quicker.

Quiet

Before you start training "Quiet!" your dog must understand a "Speak!" cue, see part 2.

Start by cueing your dog to "Speak!" only reward this with a soft verbal cue (eventually you will phase this out, but for the moment you do not want to devalue your "Speak!" behaviour).

As your dog <u>stops</u> barking say "Quiet!", "Enough!", "Shhh!" or another verbal cue you would like to use and reward with a higher value reward.

If you would like to use a hand signal as well, such as bringing your finger to your lips, you can add this in at the same time as adding your verbal cue in this training instance, just be sure you are ready to give that reward.

This is teaching your dog that the "Quiet!" cue is much more valuable than the "Speak!" cue. Can you see how this will now work?

There is of course no reason for you to stop working on your 3Ds with the "Speak!" cue, just remember to work it during a separate training session to your "Quiet!" cue. This is because increasing 3Ds on a behaviour means that it needs reinforcing and rewarding and you want to retain the higher value on the "Quiet!" cue. Therefore, when training the "Speak!" cue, always use a lower value reward than for "Quiet!".

REMEMBER

No matter what you are teaching your dog, if you move at a pace they are comfortable with you will be fine. Gradually build up the 3Ds and, should things go wrong, reduce the 3Ds a little to a point where your dog is more successful.

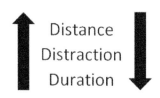

Distance
Distraction
Duration

Jo's Jargon Buster
(In alphabetical order)

While all these fancy dog training words can seem a little daunting, you need to understand them to be able to train your dog.

Capturing
This is catching a behaviour when it just happens to be done, rather like pressing the button of your camera to capture a picture.

Counter Conditioning
Changing your dog's response towards a stimulus, for example when the doorbell goes instead of barking at the door, your dog goes to their bed.

Cue
This is what you call a behaviour. Do not say the cue to your dog until they understand the position you are asking them to get into.

Desensitisation
Gradual exposure to a stimulus at a low level.

Hierarchy of rewards
This is knowing what your dogs likes, loves, hates and everything in between and in what order. So, does your dog prefer cheese to hotdog? Would your dog rather have a ball than a piece of cheese? If you know what your dog likes the most, you can use this to your advantage when training.

Jackpots
When I talk about a jackpot, I do not mean this is giving a huge handful of rewards in one go, this is just seen as one reward from your dog's perspective. Think of a jackpot as when a few coins drop out, then a few more, then a few more. Treat the same way, one reward, then another, and another and another, keep going. Your dog needs to feel like they have won the lottery for a recall. Keep your rewards small, do not give them a whole cocktail sausage for each repetition, your dog will not know whether they are having a whole cocktail sausage or just a teeny piece of one. Your dog will remember that recalls earn a massive pay out every time and that is what you want. Vary what they get, if you give only one cookie, they will take the cookie and run off again or that smell in the bushes may just be much better than that one cookie. Jackpots can be made up of rewards, play, petting and praise - make them the best thing ever!

Lure

With a reward in your hand show it to your dog and guide them into position by moving your hand. As your dog moves into the position (or a close approximation of the position if they are just learning it) give them the reward. Do not use a verbal cue for this position until your dog is able to do it all the time.

Removing the lure

Once your dog is consistently offering the position, remove the food lure from your hand. Still request the position with your hand signal and when your dog is in position reward from the other hand. At this point start adding the verbal cue.

Mark

You can use a verbal marker or a clicker to indicate to your dog at what moment they did something that earnt them a reward.

Proofing

Practicing the behaviours that you want to make them strong in a variety of settings, with distractions, by always increasing one of the 3Ds. Just make sure you do not jump from a level one sit to a level ten distraction (that is only setting up you and your dog for failure) work through levels one at a time and only move on to a harder level when you are certain that your dog will carry out that behaviour. For example, if you want me to sit, great I can sit on a chair no problem at all, but what happens if you move me to level ten immediately and Gary Barlow walks into the room! Do you think I would stay sat on the chair if you have not offered me enough that there is more value to stay in the chair?

Reinforcement

This is strengthening a behaviour/action with a reward. This can be a reward you provide or your dog finds for themselves.

Release word

I like to use "OK", but you can use any word you like. A release word lets your dog know it is alright for them to move from their current position.

Reward

This can be anything your dog likes. I refer to using a reward or food reward in the book. However, if your dog is not motivated by food then you can use what motivates them. A play with a ball, a game of tuggy or even a simple smile and tickle under the chin. No matter what your dog enjoys, it can be used as a reward.

Sweet Spot
The area in between thresholds, the perfect place to do some training.

Threshold
The line in the sand that is crossed, whether under or over. Under threshold is feeling tired, depressed, unmotivated. Over threshold is feeling hyper, angry, wound up.

Trigger Stacking
When triggers (whether they are known or unknown) appear after each other too frequently to allow recovery from the previous trigger/s off to over threshold land you go. No valid learning can take place, it is time for some enrichment and a cuppa.

Variable rate of reinforcement
If reinforcement is received randomly it makes behaviours stronger, so if learnt behaviours (whether you want them or not) are rewarded in this way then is makes them harder to change.

APPENDIX B

Get your geek on

More information if you want it

What is Marking?

I am not talking about your dog having a pee where another dog has. Marking is saying to your dog... *"Right there pup! That is exactly what I'm looking for!"*

Having a marker cue can help you when training your dog, you may wish to use a clicker, but these are easily forgotten or can get too cumbersome if you have rewards, a lead etc. Therefore, unless you are already skilled with a clicker, then I would not worry about adding one. You can just as easily **"mark"** a behaviour with a verbal cue.

Chose a verbal marker cue that comes to **YOU** naturally! If others are also working with your dog, they can have different cues if that suits them better, your dog will understand multiple marker cues. However, depending on the amount of training and reinforcement they receive for a marker, will depend on how much value it has. So, the more you use a marker and reward it, the more value it will have. Remember, you get out what you put in.

When choosing a verbal marker keep it short and sweet, some examples are below:
Yes
Yip
Good
Nice

If you are new to using a marker, then once you have decided on what you will use you need to charge it up with some value. Remember, saying this marker to your dog at the moment means **nothing** so let's charge it up.

Say your marker word and drop a nice reward in front of your dog. Now do it again, and again, and again and again.

Practise this as much as you can. Ask your dog for a behaviour they know, as they do the behaviour **mark** it and drop a reward.

What you are doing is teaching your dog that when they hear this marker word, whatever it is, they were doing something that means wonderful things are about to happen.

As a final note, you must ensure that every time you say this word to your dog, you reward it. Otherwise, the marker word will be devalued and we do not want this.

What is Reinforcement?

Without getting into the nitty gritty of all the science, the absolute basics you must understand are...

> If a behaviour is reinforced, it **will** continue.
>
> If a behaviour is not reinforced, it **will not** continue

Reinforcement is what happens during or just after a behaviour, essentially the consequence for the behaviour. So, the behaviour is **marked,** and the **reward** is what is physically given for carrying out a behaviour.

Reinforcing and rewarding are closely linked, the more a behaviour is reinforced and rewarded, the more it will happen.

So what rewards are best to use when training your dog?

Well sadly, this is not for you to decide! Therefore, you need to know what your dog likes and dislikes as, like us, they are not all the same.

For instance, if you were paid £1 to go to work one day, you would probably not bother getting out of bed the next morning. But if you were paid £1000 an hour, that would be worth getting out of bed in the morning for!

The same applies for your dog. If you are trying to reward them with something they do not want, your dog is not likely to want to do the behaviour again.

One of my dogs does not like cheese -crazy I know - so if I try to train him with cheese, he looks at me in disgust and walks away. Have I rewarded him for a good job done? **NO!**

Therefore, it is **vital** that what you have on offer for your dog is something they want.

Rewards do not have to all be food related if you have a dog that is not fussed by food, anything your dog wants can be used as a reinforcer. Ensure that whatever you dog wants is available to them.

You can use your voice to encourage your dog if they are doing something you want them to continue doing.

For instance, you can say
"Oh, you're such a good pup, I love you so much!"
"There's a good pup, let's keep going!"
"Clever pup, nearly, you're doing so well!"

Variable Rate of Reinforcement

Why are fruit machines bad for you and your dog?

So why are fruit machines bad? I will step away from the obvious that it's gambling, but what do fruit machines do? They keep us coming back for more. We might pop £1 in while we are passing and then £5 drops out! We may put another £1 in as we did not lose the last one, nothing comes out, but we have a little hope and we put another £1 in. Then £1 drops out! So, we keep playing in the hope of more rewards (watch out this is a slippery slope).

The same applies to your dog for unwanted behaviours. If your dog is getting reinforced and rewarded for a behaviour on the odd occasion (the same way as a fruit machines pay out randomly) then what this will actually do is make the behaviour **stronger!**

The jargon term for this is a **variable rate of reinforcement** and this will make behaviours stronger and less likely to stop. So, when I say set your dog up to succeed, I am not saying it just to encourage you to be your dog's cheerleader, I am saying it because it is truly **vital** in solving problem behaviours.

If your dog gets to practise an unwanted behaviour at all, it has been reinforced so it will continue. It is as simple as that. If your dog gets to randomly practice an unwanted behaviour this will create a behaviour that is so strong that you are less likely to eliminate it.

There will be the odd occasion where you will beat yourself up mentally for slipping up, but please don't, we are only human!

We are not infallible and these things will happen. Just get back on the horse, reflect on what went wrong and get back on track.

Time for a bit of R&R – that is Reinforcement and Reward in this case

The aim of this extra information is not to bore you with the science and jargon, but to provide you with a little more knowledge and understanding about how you can get the most out of your dog training.

Reinforcement is what happens during or just after a behaviour. The **reward** is what is physically given for carrying out a behaviour.

For example, if you ask your dog to sit and they do, you will **mark** your approval with a word or a clicker which is the **reinforcement** and follow this up with something your dog wants, which is the **reward**. Positive reinforcement in all its glory.

NOTE: The **marker** MUST be understood (conditioned) by your dog, so they know that when they hear it, the **reward** is next. This is known as a **conditioned reinforcer** - we have conditioned something to mean that a reward is coming.
Another example, but with a delay between the reinforcement and reward, is if your dog is behaving nicely next to you in the living room and you have just finished a telephone call, you may verbally praise them by saying "You're such a good pup, I'm going to get you a treat from the kitchen." which is **reinforcement** and then, when you give them the treat, they have received their **reward**.

I understand that this must sound very technical, but the most important thing I am trying to put across to you is how to understand what your dog sees as and what you can use as, a **REWARD.**

It is vital that you <u>know</u> what your dog likes because there is no point giving out dog a reward that they do not like. If you do, you will reduce the likelihood of the desired behaviour recurring.

For example: If I asked you to you sit, and you did, I praise you verbally with a *"Well done, that's amazing!"* and offer you some Marmite on toast. As a guess, if I offered Marmite on toast as a reward to my students, only 50% of them would be happy and the other 50% would not be* (yougov.co.uk, 2011). Therefore, if I asked the same students to sit again, would the 50%

that do not like Marmite sit? Chances are they will not, as they do not find value in Marmite on toast (for the record I would sit all day long for Marmite on toast, I'm a lover, not a hater).

*Actual Marmite figures are 33% love it, 33% hate it and 27% neither love or hate it.

https://yougov.co.uk/topics/consumer/articles-reports/2011/09/23/love-it-hate-it-its-official [accessed May 2020]

Hierarchy of Rewards

This is just a fun little experiment you can do with your dog to find out what they like.

What would happen if the tone of my *"Well done, that's amazing!"* sounded sarcastic to you? Would you repeat the behaviour? Not likely as that verbal marker does not guarantee you are going to get a reward.

Therefore, you must be 100% sure that your dog is enjoying whatever you are offering as a reward, and you must ensure that they know you have marked a desired behaviour. Therefore, here is a little more for you to think about:

Rewards are not always about food! Not all dogs are motivated by food. Make sure that you know **all** the things your dog likes and loves.

It could be they like chicken, but they love cheese and dislike ham.

Your dog may love a tennis ball, but hate a tug toy, how do they feel about a squeaky tennis ball? Do they love it more or less than a non-squeaking ball?

Your dog may dislike a scratch on the head but love a tickle behind the ear.

It could even be a life reward like sniffing, swimming or rolling in the grass, if your dog enjoys it, it is a reward.

One final example to clarify this. If you were to offer me a piece of red velvet cake or some cheese and crackers, I would choose the cheese and crackers. However, if you were to offer me lemon drizzle cake or cheese and crackers, I would choose the lemon drizzle cake. The same applies for your dog, they will enjoy lots of different rewards and these may not always be food related or have the same value.

Every dog will have a different value for different rewards, it is their choice

Therefore, it is your job to get to know your dog and find out what they like, you cannot assume that they like something. Spend the time on a little experiment.

- Write down all the rewards that *you think* your dog likes in the table I have provided in appendix C.
- List different foods, toys, games, different physical touches, different words, do they like to lick your face. Anything at all that you think your dog finds rewarding - add it to the list.
- Choose a behaviour that your dog knows well, such as "paw" and see how many times they will do this behaviour in one minute.
- Make a note of this number.

Then do this again and see how many repetitions of the behaviour you get with each different reward you have listed.

- If the number of repetitions within that minute is under the " normal" number, then remove this from your list of rewards
- If the number of repetitions within that minute is over the " normal" number, then keep this on your list of rewards

PLEASE NOTE

Work through your list gradually, not all in one training session or one day as you do not want to bore your dog or devalue a behaviour.

APPENDIX C

Tables

You can also find printable resources at
www.paws-itivity.co.uk/downloads

What does your dog like?

List everything you think your dog finds rewarding

Reward	Give the reward a score out of 10 that reflects the value to your dog 1 = likes but not fussed 5 = Yeah I like that 10= Yeah, yeah, give me! I'll do anything for that
e.g. Tennis Ball Cheese Tug Toy Chicken	5 2 7 9

Hierarchy of rewards

Using the list you made, do an experiment with each reward and see if a behaviour stays the same, increases or decreases. Knowing what your dog likes best means that you can use the rewards with the most value for more tricky training scenarios. For example, there is no point using boring biscuits (unless these are your dog's favourite) when you want to get that perfect recall for the first time on a busy beach.

By knowing what our dogs like, we can ensure that we use a reward suitable for the behaviour we are for. If we do an amazing job but do not get recognition for it, are we likely to perform that well again?

Low	Medium	High
e.g. Rope toy Plain biscuit Smile/eye contact	e.g. Tennis ball Chicken Silly talk	e.g. Squeaky toy Roast beef Playing and dancing around

Use this table to note down training sessions, unusual barking, known barking times/issues.

You can download a copy from www.paws-itivity.co.uk/downloads

	Morning	Midday	Evening
Monday			
Tuesday			
Wednesday			
Thursday			
Friday			
Saturday			
Sunday			

Basic Behaviours Progress Record

Score the below behaviours out of five

(one being that your dog does not know the behaviour, three being your dog will do the behaviour around a little excitement, five being your dog will do the behaviour around a lot of excitement)

If you have more than one dog complete this for each dog

Complete at the start of your training

	1	2	3	4	5
Sit					
Down					
Recall					
Reflex to Name					
Hand Touch					
Eye Contact					
Settle					
Speak					

For completion through your training to track improvements

	1	2	3	4	5
Sit					
Down					
Recall					
Reflex to Name					
Hand Touch					
Eye Contact					
Settle					
Speak					

I hope that you have found the training principles in this book useful, not just for excessive barking, but for retraining any other unwanted behaviours.

Remember…

Strive for progress, not perfection

About the author

Jo has always been passionate about animals, from a young age she had hamsters, guinea pigs, rabbits and even stick insects. She started training her guinea pigs to tackle small obstacles for food rewards at a young age and would spend most of her time in "Ginky Corner".

As Jo grew, so did her love of and size of animals and her focus turned to dogs and horses. Jo attended college to work with horses, but in her early twenties, after a nasty fall, she chose to concentrate full time on dogs.

In her twenties, Jo worked in accounts but spent her spare time exploring the countryside with her Labrador Max. She then began assisting at local dog training classes in the evenings and her passion for pooches grew!

By the time Jo was in her thirties, dogs were a way of life: anything worth involved dogs – a passion and an obsession.

Having completed more training and courses completed than you can wag a tail at, the natural move was to become a full-time dog trainer.

Jo's passion for helping as many dogs and owners as possible, as well as her natural teaching ability, made her dreams a reality.

Jo now runs a successful training business in West Sussex where she has helped thousands of dogs and owners. Jo currently has four dogs which are all trained in agility, scentwork, trick training and, there is more to come.

Need more help?

Facebook Group

If you would like access to the original Ban the Bark Facebook group with all the live chats then please send an email with your purchase information to jo@paws-itivity.co.uk and you will be provided with access to the group.

YouTube Videos

These can be found via my website www.paws-itivity.co.uk/btb
Password – **BanTBark**

Downloads available from my website

www.paws-itivity.co.uk/downloads

Does your dog bark excessively at home?
Is it causing you problems?

Would you like to find a way to start resolving this noisy problem?

Ban the Bark has been designed for dog owners that want to silence this noisy habit.

You may have tried asking fellow dog owners what they do or looked for articles or blogs online, scouring social media and video sites for an answer. You may have now tried so many things that your head is spinning and you feel overwhelmed, which is not helping the situation. I want you to be comfortable and confident, knowing that all you need to do is learn some simple skills to teach your dog and put you on the path to a quieter life.

This book will only promote the use of force free and positive methods of reinforcement. Under no circumstance should any aversive training be carried out. The book is set out in easy-to-understand units for you to work through at a pace you are comfortable and successful with. Take your time, this is a marathon and not a sprint. Although I try to keep this book as simple as possible, there are some additional areas of extra explanation which have been included as additional reference points and information for those that wish to know more. You can, of course skip these bits and stick to the training. It is not necessary for you to understand why I am suggesting you do something; I have just provided additional information as many owners like to understand the reasons behind the methods.

Please note that this book is not for any dog that is barking due to health or anxiety issues. If you are unsure why your dog has started barking so much, then your first point of call should be to your veterinarian.